# Ponies of the world
## Coloring Book

## John Green

DOVER PUBLICATIONS, INC.
Mineola, New York

# NOTE

A pony is a small horse, less than 14 hands high. A "hand" is 4 inches, or about 10 centimeters, long. The height is determined by measuring the distance from the highest point of a horse's withers (the ridge between the shoulder bones) in a perpendicular line to the ground. Polo ponies and cow ponies are often several inches taller than the official height limit, yet they are still called ponies.

Ponies, which tend to be sturdier and hardier than horses, often live in the wild where they endure harsh weather and survive on meager diets. Because ponies are usually gentle and intelligent, for centuries people have used them for work and pleasure. The pony's small size and generally docile disposition has made it an ideal mount for children. In some parts of the world, however, adults ride ponies and use them to carry or pull heavy loads.

## Color glossary

**bay:** reddish shades on the body; black mane, tail, and lower legs (known as points).

**black:** true black with no light areas.

**brown:** black with light areas at the muzzle, eyes, and inside of the legs.

**chestnut:** pure or reddish brown with points the same or lighter color.

**dorsal, or eel stripe:** a stripe running down a horse's neck, and along its back, sometimes to the tip of its tail; usually black, brown, or chestnut color; found mostly on dun-colored animals.

**dun:** gray-yellow with a black dorsal stripe, black mane and tail; sometimes there are zebra stripes on the legs and a crosswise stripe on the withers.

**piebald:** a horse with black and white patches over its body, sometimes including its tail.

**roan:** any color with white hairs mixed throughout, lightening the effect.

**skewbald:** a horse covered with patches of white and any color, except black.

**sorrel:** light chestnut, often with white mane and tail.

*Bibliographical Note*

*Ponies of the World Coloring Book* is a new work, first published by Dover Publications, Inc., in 1999.

*International Standard Book Number*

*ISBN-13: 978-0-486-40564-3*
*ISBN-10: 0-486-40564-8*

Manufactured in the United States by Courier Corporation
40564806
www.doverpublications.com

**Sable Island Pony.** Descended from horses that were brought to Nova Scotia from France, the Sable Island pony has roamed semi-wild since the 18th century. The harsh climate of the island has forced this pony to become incredibly hardy. Its coat may be gray, brown, black, or chestnut. If domesticated young, it is docile. It is used for riding and pulling light loads.

**Assateague and Chincoteague Ponies.** These ponies are believed to be descended from horses that survived a shipwreck in the early days of the American colonies. The island of Assateague, off the coasts of Virginia and Maryland, is uninhabited by humans. Here the ponies live in the wild. Each year, at the end of July, ponies are herded across the channel to the island of Chincoteague, where they are auctioned. Although they are known to be rebellious and stubborn, these ponies are used for riding and pulling light loads. Their coats can be almost any color, although piebald and skewbald are most common.

2

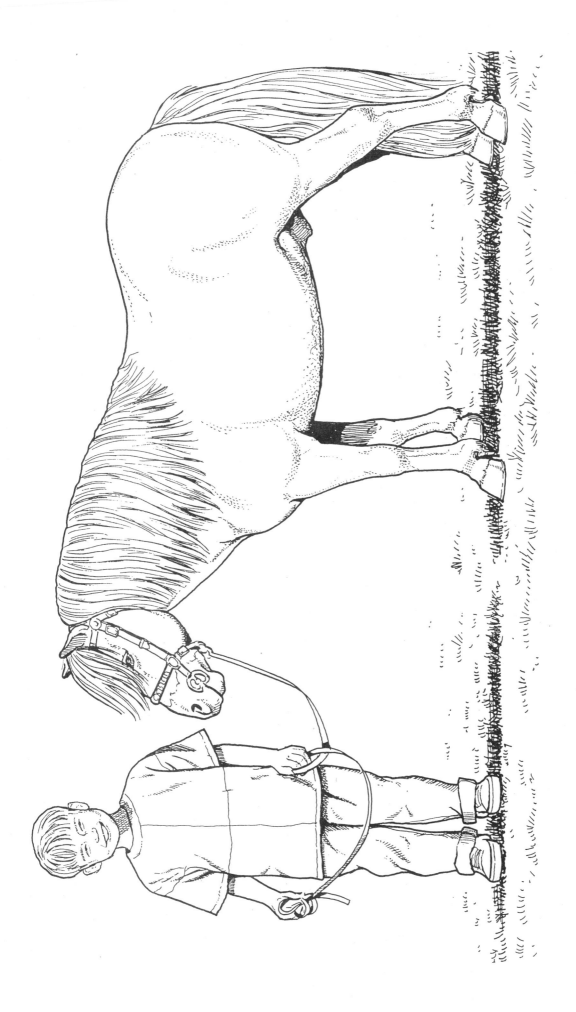

**Shetland Pony.** The Shetland pony is from the Shetland and Orkney islands, north of Scotland. While fossils suggest that this pony dates back to the Bronze Age, some experts believe that it was brought by a ship in the Spanish Armada during the 16th century. Standing 9 to 10 hands, it is one of the smallest of all ponies, and may be the strongest of all horses in relation to its size. Hearty and long lived, it is also the most popular breed. Because it can be stubborn, this pony needs firm training. Shetlands with coats that are chestnut, bay, and black are popular for show; Shetlands with piebald and skewbald coats tend to be chosen for children.

**American Shetland Pony.** As a result of different breeding conditions in the United States, the American Shetland is a lighter, more refined version of the Shetland pony from the United Kingdom.

**Pony of the Americas.** The result of breeding a Shetland pony with an Appaloosa in the 1960s, the Pony of the Americas grows to 12.1 hands. Its coat is usually a dark spotted pattern on roan or white. Versatile, swift, and an excellent jumper, this pony is popular for competition, racing, and long distance riding. It's a docile pony, ideal for children.

**Galiçeno Pony.** Descended from the Garrano, this pony was brought to Mexico by Spanish *conquistadors* in the 16th century. Today it is used in Mexico for carrying packs, draft, and farm work. Its coat may be bay, black, or chestnut, with piebald, skewbald, and albino not permitted. Known to be gentle, intelligent, and courageous, the Galiçeno has been imported to the United States since 1950 where it has proved to be a fine jumper in events for children.

**Falabella Pony.** At 34 inches high, or 86 centimeters, the Falabella pony is the smallest breed in the world. Bred by the Falabella family at their ranch near Argentina, it is docile and intelligent. It's a popular riding and harness pony for children because it is so strong for its size. Graceful and attractive, it comes in all colors.

**Connemara Pony.** The Connemara pony is an ancient Celtic breed, one of the earliest inhabitants of the British Isles. For centuries, the tough, handsome Connemara has run wild on the west coast of Ireland. With its compact body and short legs, it is known for its stamina and staying power. Docile and intelligent, it is used for riding and driving. The Connemara pony is usually gray, but may also be black, bay, brown, dun, roan, or chestnut.

**Dales Pony.** The Dales pony, a native of northern England, has a strong frame that enables it to pull heavy loads. In the 19th century, it was used to carry lead from the mines to the docks. A harness pony today, it is popular for work on small farms, especially in Scotland. Many Dales ponies are jet black, followed by bay, brown, and gray. They all have thick manes and tails.

**Dartmoor Pony.** An indigenous, mountain breed, the Dartmoor pony roams wild over the high, craggy hills of Dartmoor, in the extreme southwest of England. If handled when young, it will become an excellent riding pony, especially for a child. Small and compact, it is remarkably long lived. With its tail set high and full, the Dartmoor pony is usually black, bay, or brown.

**Fell Pony.** At the end of the 19th century, the Fell pony roamed wild over the barren moors of northern England. Like the Dales pony, the Fell pony was once used to carry lead from the mines to the docks. But while the Dales pony is now favored for carrying packs, the Fell pony is preferred for riding. Its coat is usually black, with no white markings, but it may also be dark brown, dark bay, gray, or dun.

**Exmoor Pony.** The Exmoor pony, descended from the native British wild horse, continues to roam the English moors of Cornwall, Devon, and Somerset. This pony remains small and hearty, which is thought to be its ancient, aboriginal state. If taken into captivity at a young age, and gently treated, it becomes a lovable, good mount. Its coloring, which may be brown, bay, or dun, is without white. When full grown, this pony may reach up to 12.2 hands.

13

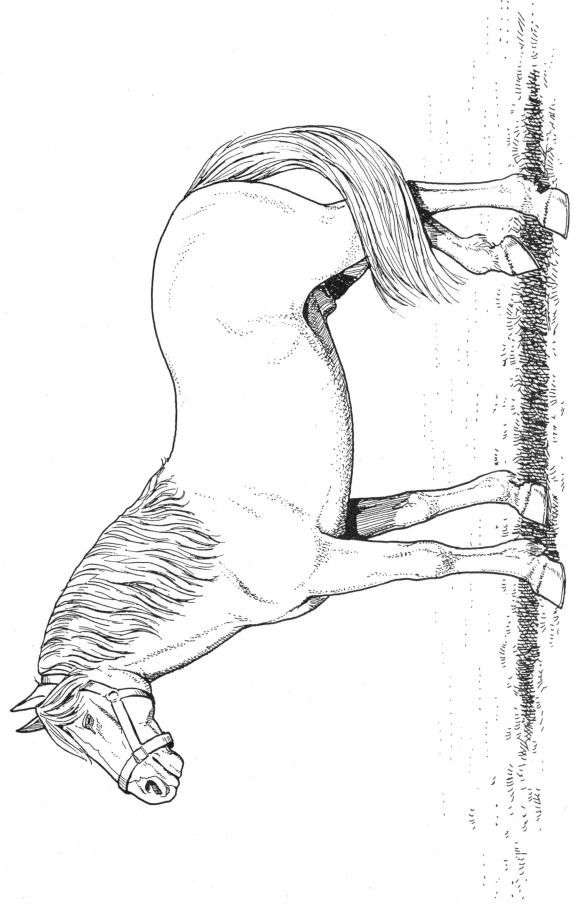

**Avelignese Pony.** Although there is little known about the earliest origins of the Avelignese pony, its history can be traced back to the Middle Ages. Originating in Italy, it is considered a breed of inter- national importance. Its coat is usually chestnut or golden, with forelock, mane, and tail a lighter shade. There is often a white blaze or understated white marking on its head.

**Welsh Pony.** The Welsh pony is a strong harness and riding pony with considerable spirit, ability, and a kind temperament. It is known for its beautiful stride, at both a trot and a gallop. In Wales it is predominantly gray, and dark, solid colors; cream and buckskin are popular in the United States. Its height may be from 12 to 13.2 hands.

**Welsh Cob.** Descended from the Welsh Mountain pony, the Welsh Cob has inherited its hardy constitution. At 14 to 15.1 hands, the Welsh Cob is ideal for carrying heavier riders, even over rough and difficult terrain. Huskier cobs are impressively strong, noted for pulling substantial loads. As with the Welsh Mountain pony, the coat of the Welsh Cob may be bay, brown, black, roan, or chestnut. It is occasionally dun or cream, but never piebald or skewbald.

**Welsh Mountain Pony.** This little pony, its height under 12 hands, still roams wild, or semi-wild, over the mountains and moors of Wales. Its intelligence, courage, endurance, and beauty make it a favorite of adults and children alike. Because of its small size, the Welsh Mountain Pony was once in great demand in coal mines. Today it is prized for riding and as foundation stock for breeding children's ponies. The dominant coat color is gray, followed by brown, chestnut, and many other colors. Only piebald and skewbald are not allowed.

**Camargue Pony.** This pony, which lives in the wilds of the Camargue, the salt marsh delta of the Rhône in France, remains unchanged since Roman times. *Guardiens,* or cowboys, ride them in pursuit of the wild black bulls that are exported to the bullrings of Spain.

The coat of the Camargue is usually gray, with bay or brown occurring rarely. Facing extinction towards the middle of the 20th century, this breed has had its own register since 1967.

**Palomino Pony.** The Palomino is registered by color because it does not yet breed true to type. Cortez, in Mexico in 1519, presented a horse of this color to Juan de Palomino. Known today as "the golden horse of the West," Palominos were rediscovered in 1848, after the Mexican War, when the United States took possession of California. Standing 14 to 16 hands, the Palomino is used for riding, driving, and stock work. The pony version is found only in Britain.

**Haflinger Pony.** Originally from the Tyrol, the Haflinger pony is a mountain horse who carries its head close to the ground as it climbs. Strong and sure-footed, it excels at carrying and pulling heavy loads, and has been employed in the mountains to work in forestry and agriculture. Its average height is under 14 hands; its color is usually dark bay or black.

**Dolmen Pony.** The Dolmen pony, from Westphalia, is bred on the estate of the Duke of Croy. The only native German pony, it is excellent for riding. The Dolmen pony stands at 12.3 hands with coat colors that are black, brown, or dun.

**Konik Pony.** Konik, which means "small horse" in Polish, refers to several native breeds in Poland. With Arabic and Celtic ancestors, this pony is valued for its stamina, hardiness, and speed. A very popular type of Konik pony comes from the Baltic region where it does agricultural work. The Konik is a mid-sized, good-natured pony whose coat color may be palomino, gray, or blue dun, usually with a dorsal stripe.

**Hucul Pony.** The Hucul has roamed the wilds of Poland's Carpathians for centuries, retaining its primitive features. Descended from the Tarpan, the Hucul was first bred formally in the 19th century. It is solidly built, standing 12 to 13 hands. Hardy and undemanding, it is used for pulling and carrying light loads, as well as for farm work. The most common colors are bay, palomino, dun, mouse dun, and gray.

23

**Sorraia Pony.** One of the first ponies to be domesticated, the Sorraia is strong and tractable enough to carry packs, to herd, and to work in agriculture. Standing about 13 hands, the Sorraia pony comes from Portugal, where it lives in the wild. Changes in its natural habitat now threaten its existence. Its coat colors may be dun, gray, or palomino, with a dorsal stripe down its back, and zebra markings on its legs.

24

**Tarpan Pony.** With origins dating back to the Ice Age, the Tarpan is the ancestor of all the lightly-built breeds now in existence. Today, herds of Tarpan ponies roam wild in the forests of Poland. They are not thought to be purebred, however, because the last true Tarpan died in captivity in 1887. Standing at about 13 hands, they are brave, independent, and difficult to train. The Tarpan's coat may be mouse dun, yellow dun, or palomino. It has a black dorsal stripe down the center of its back, a black mane and tail, and black or zebra-marked legs.

**Garrano Pony.** Ponies of this very old breed resemble horses depicted in cave paintings from the Paleolithic era. Originating in Portugal, along the Spanish border, until recently the Garrano pony was used for traditional trotting races. Today it is utilized as a riding and pack pony, and for farm work. A small pony, it stands from 10 to 12 hands and has a quiet, docile temperament. Its coat is chestnut.

**Fjord Pony.** Retaining the characteristics of its Ice Age ancestors, the Norwegian Fjord pony was used by Vikings during times of war, as shown in rock and cave paintings. Present day heavy draft breeds in western Europe are thought to be descended from this strong, stocky pony. Standing about 13 to 14 hands, it is used today as a riding and pack pony, and for light draft and farm work. Usually dun-colored with a black dorsal stripe and a black and silver mane, the Fjord pony is gentle, but stubborn.

**Iceland Pony.** The Iceland pony is descended from two types of ponies that were brought to Iceland by settlers; the Norwegians arrived in 874, followed soon after by the Irish. For a thousand years, this pony provided the only means of transportation on Iceland. Short and stocky, it is extremely hardy, with exceptionally sharp eyesight. Because the Iceland pony is born with a unique homing ability, there is a custom of turning a pony loose after a long trip; it usually returns home within 24 hours. Although gentle and friendly, the Iceland pony is stubborn, independent, and difficult to train.

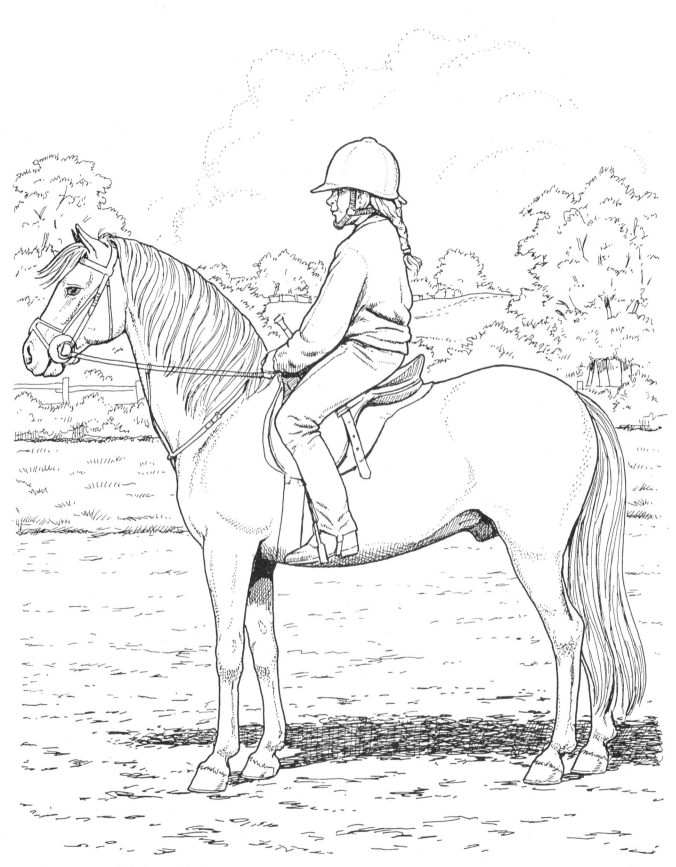

**Caspian Pony.** Archaeological finds in Iran suggest that ancestors of the Caspian pony may have been domesticated by the Mesopotamians around 3000 B.C. Thought to have become extinct by the 10th century, in 1965, a number of these ponies were discovered living in Iran's Elburz Mountains and along the Caspian Sea. This docile pony is a good riding horse and an excellent jumper. Its coat may be chestnut, bay, or gray; a few have white markings on their heads and legs.

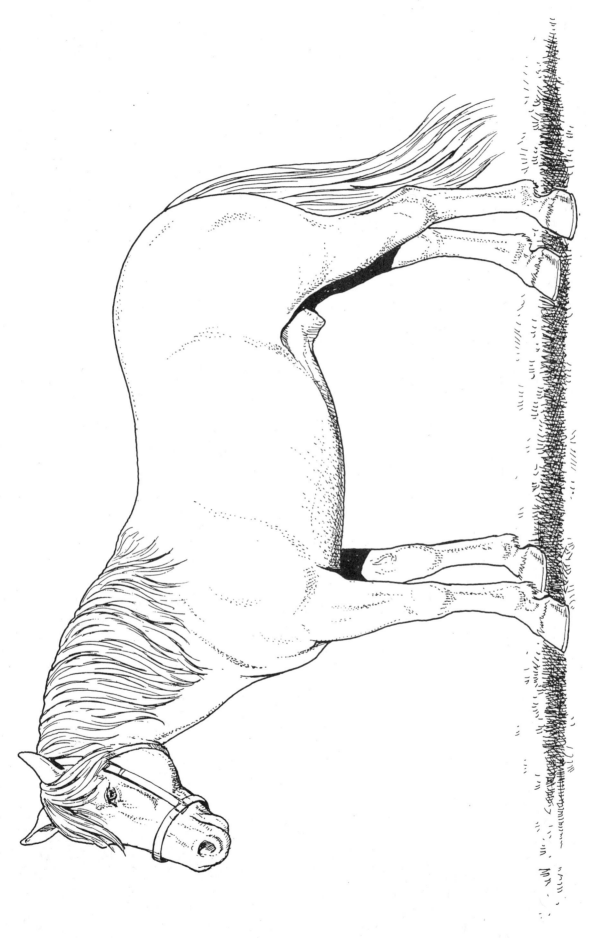

**Bosnian Pony.** This durable pony is so important for farm work that its breeding is closely monitored by the state. It is also used for carrying packs, light draft, and riding. Standing at 12 to 14 hands, the Bosnian pony may be bay, dun, brown, black, or chestnut.

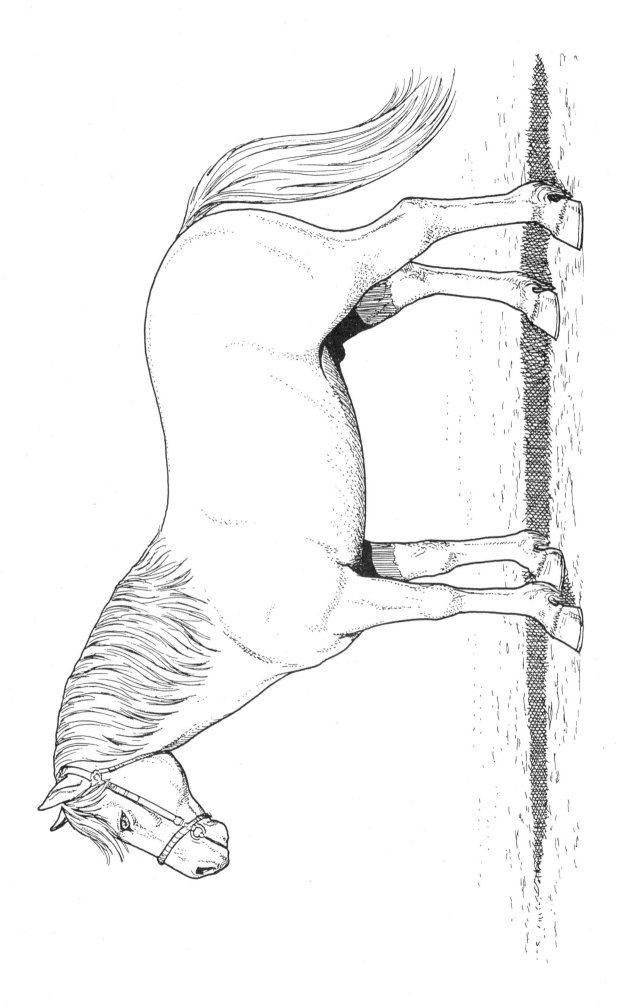

**Spiti Pony.** From the Himalayas in India, the Spiti is a rugged mountain pony that thrives only in the cold climate. The ponies carry huge loads up and down winding mountain paths. Usually tied together in a long line, the ponies walk with their heads down. Despite appearing to be half asleep, they are always alert enough to nip at whoever or whatever gets in their way. About 12 hands high, the Spiti often has a gray coat.

31

**New Forest Pony.** The New Forest pony roams the 60,000 acre New Forest in southern England which, in reality, is a sparse grazing land of scrub and heather. In order to survive under such desolate conditions, these ponies have become frugal eaters who can endure harsh weather. The present breed was developed in the mid-19th century when Queen Victoria sent an Arab stallion to live in the New Forest for 8 years. Intelligent, courageous, and willing, the New Forest pony is used for light draft work, polo, and other equestrian competitions. The most common coat color for this pony is gray or brown. All colors are permitted, except piebald and skewbald.

**Skyros Pony.** From the Greek island of Skyros, this pony is one of the few breeds that has not interbred. Quiet and trustworthy, it is used as a pack animal, for farm work, and as a riding pony for children. Considered unattractive in its wild state, its appearance improves greatly with proper food and care. Its height is approximately 10 hands. Its coat may be dun, brown, or gray.

**Zemaituka Pony.** This pony, from western Lithuania, has ancient beginnings. Renowned for its staying power and ability to survive hardship, it has been mentioned as far back as the 13th century when it carried warriors on raids deep into Russia. Today it is used for farm work and light draft. From 13 to 15 hands high, it may be dun color with a light tail and mane, as well as mouse color or bay. A dorsal or eel stripe extends to its tail.

**Bashkirsky Pony.** A very old breed from the Baltic region, Bashkirsky mares have long been milked for koumiss, a medicinal and alcoholic drink. Standing 13 to 14 hands tall, this strong pony is used for riding and light draft. There are two types of Bashkirsky ponies; the smaller and lighter mountain type is better suited to riding, while the heavier, steppes type is used for pulling a troika (a Russian vehicle with 3 horses abreast). Its coat is usually bay, chestnut, dun, or palomino.

**Mongolian Pony.** Of ancient origin, this pony is kept and bred in huge numbers by nomad Mongolian tribes who do not provide them with any special care or food. The region where they live is extremely inhospitable, so the ponies that adapted over the centuries have become hardy. The most valued Mongolian pony is the Wuchumutsin who has the advantage of being reared in fertile pastures. The coat of the Mongolian pony may be brown, black, dun or palomino.

36

**Viatka Pony.** Originating in the Baltic states, this breed is descended from the Konik pony. Energetic and willing, it is used for light farm work. Because it has a short stride, the Viatka pony does especially well on snow covered ground. Its coat may be bay, gray, or roan. A coat that is dun, mouse dun, or palomino is usually accompanied by an eel stripe, zebra markings on the legs, a black mane and tail.

**Batak Pony.** Originating in Indonesia and Sumatra, the Batak pony averages about 11.3 hands, although some reach the height of 12.2 hands. Bred from a native pony and an Arabian, its physique is comparatively refined and well formed. Of gentle temperament and modest needs, it is an excellent pony for agricultural and transportation work. Most have brown coats, although many are skewbald.

**Highland Pony.** The Highland pony is the largest and the strongest of Great Britain's moor land and mountain breeds. Found in the highlands of Scotland and a few adjacent islands, its origins can be traced back to the Ice Age. With a strong and sturdy build, it has been used in the mountains to hunt deer. Its coat may be black, brown, dun, gray, and many other colors.

**Manipur Pony.** The Manipur pony is mentioned as far back as the 7th century when the king of Manipur, in India, introduced polo which was played on ponies bred in his state. Although polo had long been known in Asia, English colonials first saw polo being played in India during the mid-19th century and introduced it in Europe. The quick, maneuverable Manipur pony has a coat that is usually bay, brown, gray, or chestnut.

**Hackney Pony.** First bred in England in the 1860s, the Hackney pony is a smaller edition of the Hackney horse. A high stepper with a graceful stride, the Hackney pony was once used to pull farmers to market. Today this handsome pony is often seen jumping in the show ring, a sport at which it excels. The pony has a long neck, good shoulders, and a compact body. Its colors are usually bay, brown, or black.

42

**Gotland Pony.** Since the Stone Age, this Swedish pony has run wild on the island of Gotland in the Baltic Sea. It is sometimes called "Skogsruss," which means "little horse in the woods," or "little goat," because it is so sure-footed. Although this hardy pony tends to be obstinate, it is used for light farm work, in trotting races, and as a children's pony. Standing from 12 to 13 hands high, its coat may be bay, brown, black, chestnut, gray, dun, palomino, or mouse dun.

43

**Rocky Mountain Pony.** Bred by Sam Tuttle of Stout Springs, Kentucky, this new breed was first registered in 1986. Calm and kind, this pony is sure-footed over rough ground. Of Spanish origin, it can measure up to 14.3 hands high. It's an all around pony that is a good choice for work on the farm, in the harness, or with a saddle.

# INDEX OF PONIES